Beyond Procrastination: Turning 'I'll Do It Later' Into Immediate Action

Copyright © 2024 Reginaldo Osnildo
All rights reserved.

PRESENTATION

INTRODUCTION TO THE SYMBOLISM OF 'LATER I WILL DO IT'

UNDERSTANDING PROCRASTINATION

IMPACT OF PROCRASTINATION

PROCRASTINATION AND ANXIETY

TIME MANAGEMENT STRATEGIES

SETTING CLEAR GOALS

THE POWER OF HABIT

PRIORITIZATION TECHNIQUES

CREATING AN ENVIRONMENTAL ENVIRONMENT

THE ROLE OF MOTIVATION

TOOLS AND RESOURCES AGAINST PROCRASTINATION

MINDFULNESS AND SELF-AWARENESS

OVERCOMING PERFECTIONISM

SMALL STEPS TO BIG CHANGES

THE IMPACT OF DEADLINES

BUILDING EMOTIONAL RESILIENCE

FEEDBACK AND SUPPORT

LEARNING FROM MISTAKES

NUTRITION AND EXERCISE

MEDITATION AND RELAXATION

CELEBRATING SUCCESSES

DISCONNECTING TO RECONNECT

STARTING WORK RITUALS

DEALING WITH GUILT

TOWARDS ACTION

REGINALDO OSNILDO

PRESENTATION

If you're holding this book, chances are you've said to yourself, "I'll do it later" more times than you can count. In today's fast-paced world, finding the motivation to start — and more importantly, keep going — can feel like a constant battle against time, energy, and, most of all, our own will. This is where **"Beyond Procrastination: Turning 'I'll Do It Later' Into Immediate Action"** comes in as your new ally.

This book is an invitation not only to understand what's behind your tendency to procrastinate, but also to completely transform your approach to everyday tasks and challenges. With it, you will discover that procrastination is not just a bad habit, but a complex behavioral pattern that can be dismantled and rebuilt in a productive and positive way.

Throughout this book, I bring my updated perspective on proven techniques and new strategies adapted for the contemporary challenges you face. Each chapter has been carefully crafted to offer deep insights and practical tools that will help you shift your mindset from "I can do it later" to "I'll do it now." We'll address the psychological causes, the impacts on your personal and professional life, and, most importantly, how you can overcome the barriers that prevent you from being the most productive version of yourself.

With accessible language and applicable tips, this book is dedicated to you, who want to not just dream, but achieve. We have prepared a path full of practical exercises, reflections and techniques that will transform the way you act and think. And at the end of each chapter, an invitation to the next, ensuring that your journey of learning and action is continuous and engaging.

Get ready to explore the symbolism of " **I'll do it later** " in the next chapter, where we dive into the psychological and behavioral implications of procrastination. Are you ready to take the first step towards a life of achievement? Let's turn intention into action together.

Accept the invitation. Your journey beyond procrastination starts now.

Yours sincerely

Reginaldo Osnildo

INTRODUCTION TO THE SYMBOLISM OF 'LATER I WILL DO IT'

Procrastination is often misinterpreted as simple laziness or poor time management. However, you may have already realized that postponing tasks goes far beyond that; It is a complex phenomenon, full of meanings and symbolism that shape our behavior and our daily choices. In this chapter, we will explore the psychological and behavioral implications of procrastination, helping you better understand this very human and challenging behavior.

THE HIDDEN MEANING OF 'LATER I'LL DO IT'

When we say " **I'll do it later** ", we are often expressing more than a simple decision to postpone a task. This act may be a reflection of several underlying issues, such as fear of failure, perfectionism, or even a form of resistance against external or internal pressures. Every time you choose not to do something right away, you are also choosing to protect yourself from something that, on some level, causes discomfort or anxiety.

THE PSYCHOLOGICAL ROOTS OF PROCRASTINATION

Procrastination is deeply rooted in our psyche. It is often an emotional response to a perceived threat – the fear of not measuring up, the fear of judgment from others, or even the fear of succeeding, which could raise expectations and pressures on us. Understanding these fears can be the first step in overcoming the tendency to procrastinate.

THE BEHAVIORAL IMPACT

Behaviorally , procrastination can manifest itself in several ways: from avoiding specific tasks to creating excuses not to start important projects. This behavior often leads to a vicious cycle of stress, guilt and low self-esteem, as the longer we postpone, the more anxious we feel, and the more anxious we feel, the more we tend to postpone.

TRANSFORMING SYMBOLISM INTO ACTION

Understanding the symbolism behind " **I'll do it later** " is crucial to breaking the cycle of procrastination. This understanding allows you to confront not only the tasks before you, but also the fears and hesitations that accompany them. By bringing to light the psychological reasons behind procrastination, you can start working on building a new mindset, one that encourages immediate action rather than procrastination.

ARE YOU READY FOR THE NEXT STEP?

Now that we've explored the symbolic complexities and behavioral impacts of procrastination, you're better prepared to tackle the root causes of this habit. In the next chapter, " **UNDERSTANDING PROCRASTINATION** ", we will dive into the common causes and psychological factors that lead to procrastination behavior. You will discover strategies for identifying and dealing with these triggers in your daily life.

Get ready to understand not just what you're putting off, but why you're putting it off. Are you ready to continue this journey of self-knowledge and transformation? Let's unravel the mysteries of procrastination together and learn how to overcome them, step by step.

UNDERSTANDING PROCRASTINATION

Procrastinating is a common behavior, but have you ever wondered why exactly you put off certain tasks? This chapter is dedicated to exploring the common causes and psychological factors that lead to procrastination behavior. By understanding the root causes of procrastination, you can develop more effective strategies to combat it in your daily life.

THE ROOTS OF PROCRASTINATION

Procrastinating is not just a matter of poor time management or laziness, as many may think. In fact, it is a complex mechanism that involves several psychological components, such as fear of failure, fear of success, aversion to unpleasant tasks, and even a lack of clarity about how to start or finish a task. Let's explore these factors further:

- **Fear of failure and success:** We often postpone tasks because we fear not being up to them or, paradoxically, we fear the success they can bring. Success raises expectations and responsibilities, which can be daunting.

- **Aversion to unpleasant tasks:** Naturally, we tend to avoid tasks that we consider unpleasant or tedious. This type of procrastination is motivated by the desire to avoid emotional or physical discomfort.

- **Overload and analysis paralysis:** When we are overwhelmed, whether by the quantity or complexity of tasks, we can feel paralyzed. The inability to prioritize or decide where to start can lead to procrastination.

- **Perfectionism:** For many, the idea of not doing something perfectly is so overwhelming that they would rather do nothing than run the risk of failing.

IDENTIFYING YOUR TRIGGER

Each person has their own procrastination triggers. Identifying these triggers is the first step to controlling them. A useful technique is to keep a procrastination journal, where you write down each instance of procrastination, what you planned to do, and why you decided to put it off. Over time, patterns will emerge, providing valuable clues about your subconscious motivations.

CONFRONTATION STRATEGIES

Understanding the causes of procrastination is essential, but knowing how to tackle them is equally important. Some strategies include:

- **Division of tasks:** Break large tasks into smaller, more manageable parts to reduce feelings of overwhelm.

- **Visualization techniques:** Imagine yourself completing the task successfully. This can help reduce your fear of failure.

- **Conducive environments:** Organize your workspace to minimize distractions and create an environment that promotes efficiency.

Now that you've begun to understand the ins and outs of procrastination, you're ready to explore how it affects your personal and professional life in the next chapter, " **IMPACT OF PROCRASTINATION** ." There, we will discuss the consequences of postponement and how it can affect all aspects of your life.

Join us in the next chapter to continue this journey towards a more productive and less procrastinating life. Are you ready to see how procrastination has shaped your life and how you can start making meaningful changes? Let's go!

IMPACT OF PROCRASTINATION

Procrastination may seem like a simple habit of putting off tasks, but its repercussions go far beyond simply putting off until tomorrow what you could do today. This chapter explores the many ways in which procrastination impacts your personal and professional life, helping you understand the seriousness of this behavior and the urgency of addressing it.

PERSONAL CONSEQUENCES OF PROCRASTINATION

In personal life, procrastination can create a series of emotional and practical problems:

- **Stress and anxiety:** Procrastination often leads to an accumulation of tasks that eventually needs to be tackled, generating high levels of stress and anxiety.

- **Low self-esteem:** By constantly putting off, you may begin to feel incapable or incompetent, which negatively affects your self-image and self-esteem.

- **Compromised relationships:** The tendency to procrastinate can also affect your relationships, whether by not fulfilling commitments or by transferring the burden of your responsibilities to others.

PROFESSIONAL IMPACTS

In the workplace, the consequences of procrastination can be even more visible and harmful:

- **Reduced performance:** Procrastinating prevents you from completing your tasks on time and with the expected quality, which can affect your performance evaluation.

- **Missed opportunities:** Failure to act quickly can mean missing valuable opportunities for advancement or participation in interesting and enriching projects.

- **Professional reputation:** Being seen as someone who always leaves everything to the last minute can harm your reputation and your chances of career advancement.

THE PSYCHOLOGICAL DIMENSION

In addition to the tangible impacts, it is important to consider the deeper psychological consequences of procrastination:

- **Vicious cycles of behavior:** Procrastination can become a difficult habit to break, especially when accompanied by feelings of guilt and frustration.

- **Erosion of self-discipline:** The more you procrastinate, the more your capacity for self-discipline is eroded, making it difficult to make assertive decisions in the future.

BREAKING UP WITH PROCRASTINATION

Recognizing the impacts of procrastination is a crucial step towards overcoming it. Strategies for breaking this cycle include establishing clear routines, using time management techniques, and, above all, gradually shifting your mindset from one of procrastination to one of action.

READY TO ADVANCE?

Now that you understand the significant impacts of procrastination, it's time to take a closer look at how it is closely linked to anxiety and stress. In the next chapter, " **PROCRASTINATION AND ANXIETY** ," we'll explore how constant procrastination can not only be a result but also a cause of anxiety, and how you can manage this destructive relationship.

Are you ready to continue exploring and combating procrastination in your life? Advance to the next chapter and discover tools and insights to help you deal with procrastination-related anxiety and transform the way you face daily challenges.

PROCRASTINATION AND ANXIETY

The relationship between procrastination and anxiety is complex and bidirectional: procrastination can be both a cause and a consequence of anxiety. This chapter examines how this cycle perpetuates itself and offers effective strategies for breaking it, promoting sustainable mental well-being and productivity.

PROCRASTINATION AS A CAUSE OF ANXIETY

Procrastinating can often seem like an easy way out of avoiding stressful or challenging tasks. However, by postponing these tasks, you accumulate not only the activities, but also the stress associated with them. This can result in a significant increase in anxiety, especially as the deadline approaches.

> **- Accumulation of tasks:** The more tasks are postponed, the greater the accumulated workload, which increases stress and anxiety levels.

> **- Time pressure:** As deadlines approach, the pressure to complete tasks in less time can intensify anxiety, making it even more difficult to start or complete work.

PROCRASTINATION AS A CONSEQUENCE OF ANXIETY

On the other hand, anxiety itself can lead to procrastination. Fear of failing, not meeting expectations, or facing unpleasant tasks can make putting it off seem like a less painful option in the short term.

> **- Avoidance:** Anxiety often leads to avoidance as a coping strategy. Procrastinating becomes a way to temporarily avoid emotional discomfort.

> **- Analysis paralysis:** Anxiety can cause what is known as analysis paralysis, where you feel so overwhelmed by the options or possible outcomes of an action that you end up not taking action.

STRATEGIES TO BREAK THE CYCLE

To effectively combat procrastination and anxiety, it is essential to adopt strategies that address both aspects:

- **Efficient time management:** Use time management techniques, such as the Pomodoro Technique or the task listing method, to divide your work into manageable segments.

- **Relaxation techniques:** Practices such as meditation, breathing exercises and yoga can help reduce anxiety levels and increase your ability to focus and concentrate.

- **Gradual confrontation:** Face the tasks you fear gradually and systematically. Start with small steps to gain confidence and reduce anxiety.

Understanding the interaction between procrastination and anxiety is just the beginning. In the next chapter, " **TIME MANAGEMENT STRATEGIES** ," we'll explore detailed techniques to help you better organize your time and tasks. These tools will not only increase your productivity but also help ease anxiety related to procrastination.

Are you ready to acquire tools that will transform your daily life, reducing both procrastination and anxiety? Let's discover together how you can take control of your time and, consequently, your life.

TIME MANAGEMENT STRATEGIES

Effective time management is one of the most powerful tools in the fight against procrastination. This chapter offers a series of techniques you can implement to not only improve your time management, but also significantly increase your productivity and reduce daily stress.

WHY IS TIME MANAGEMENT CRUCIAL?

Good time management allows you to better control your daily schedule, prioritizing tasks and reducing wasted time. Not only does this improve your performance at work and at home, but it also helps reduce anxiety caused by feeling like you're always "running out of time."

EFFECTIVE TIME MANAGEMENT TECHNIQUES

- **Pomodoro Technique:** This technique involves working with total focus for periods of 25 minutes, followed by a 5-minute break. After four "pomodoros," take a longer break of 15 to 30 minutes. This method helps maintain concentration and avoid fatigue.

- **Eisenhower Method:** Also known as the Priority Matrix, this technique helps you decide on and prioritize tasks based on their urgency and importance, dividing them into four categories: doing now, deciding when to do, delegating and not doing.

- **Two-minute rule:** If a task can be done in two minutes or less, do it immediately. This avoids piling up small tasks, which can become a source of procrastination.

- **Setting clear goals and objectives:** Setting clear and achievable goals for each day, week and month can help maintain your focus and direction, reducing time spent on unproductive activities.

CREATING A DAILY ROUTINE

In addition to adopting specific techniques, establishing a daily routine can be extremely beneficial. A well-structured routine not only helps automate decisions, reducing mental load, but also ensures that essential tasks are carried out.

- **Plan your day the night before:** Take a few minutes each night to plan the next day. This may include defining key tasks to be performed and preparing necessary materials in advance.

READY FOR THE NEXT STEP?

Now that you are equipped with effective time management strategies, the next chapter, " **SETTING CLEAR GOALS** ", will help you deepen your ability to set goals that are not only realistic but also motivating. Setting clear goals is crucial to avoiding procrastination and feeling a sense of direction and purpose.

Are you ready to learn the art of setting goals effectively and transform the way you approach your tasks and projects? Let's explore together how clarity in goals can revolutionize your productivity and boost your success.

SETTING CLEAR GOALS

Setting clear and achievable goals is essential to combat procrastination and boost productivity. In this chapter, we'll explore the importance of setting well-defined goals and how this practice can help you focus your energy and organize your time effectively.

THE IMPORTANCE OF CLEAR GOALS

Clear goals provide a sense of direction and purpose. They transform broad visions into concrete, measurable steps, which is essential for maintaining motivation and commitment. Without clear goals, it is easy to get lost in less important activities, increasing the tendency to procrastinate.

HOW TO SET EFFECTIVE GOALS

For your goals to be effective, they must be SMART: Specific, Measurable, Attainable, Relevant and Timely. Let's detail each of these criteria:

- **Specific:** Your goals must be clear and specific, so that you know exactly what needs to be achieved. For example, instead of saying "I want to write more", say "I want to write a chapter a week".

- **Measurable:** There must be clear criteria to measure progress towards the goal. Knowing you're getting closer to your goal can be a powerful motivator.

- **Achievable:** Goals must be realistic and achievable within a reasonable period of time. Setting very ambitious goals can be demotivating.

- **Relevant:** Your goals should be important to you and align with your broader directions and values. A relevant goal increases personal motivation to achieve it.

- **Temporal:** Each goal must have a defined deadline, which creates a sense of urgency necessary to avoid procrastination.

TIPS FOR STAYING FOCUSED ON GOALS

- **Visualize your goals:** Create a clear picture of what achieving your goals will look like. Visualization is a powerful technique that can help you stay focused and motivated.

- **Review regularly:** Reviewing your goals regularly can help you adjust them as needed and stay on track.

- **Celebrate small victories:** Celebrate each small success along the way. This can boost your self-confidence and reinforce your commitment to bigger goals.

With your goals now well defined and a framework for achieving them in hand, the next chapter, " **THE POWER OF HABIT** ", will explore how to develop daily habits that support your goals and combat procrastination. Learning to establish and maintain good habits can be the key to turning your intentions into effective, lasting actions.

Are you ready to dive even deeper and turn your goals into consistent realities? Let's discover together how habits can shape your journey towards success and productivity.

THE POWER OF HABIT

Turning intentions into effective and consistent actions is one of the biggest struggles against procrastination. This chapter explores how developing daily habits can not only help with time management and achieving goals, but also help with building a routine that promotes productivity and overall well-being.

THE IMPORTANCE OF HABITS

Habits are automatic behaviors that play a crucial role in our daily lives, influencing almost everything we do. When you develop habits that align your actions with your goals, you reduce the need to make decisions and employ constant will, which reduces mental fatigue and procrastination.

HOW TO FORM NEW HABITS

Forming new habits can be challenging, but it is entirely possible with strategic approaches. Here are some essential steps to help you build lasting habits:

- **Start small:** Choose a new habit that is so simple you can't say no. For example, instead of trying to exercise for an hour every day, start with five minutes a day.

- **Add to the existing one:** Link the new habit to an existing routine. For example, if you want to start meditating, do it right after brushing your teeth in the morning.

- **Positive reinforcement:** Give yourself an immediate reward when you perform the new habit. This can reinforce the behavior and increase the likelihood of repetition.

- **Consistency:** The key to habit formation is consistency. The more you repeat an action, the more it becomes automatic.

CHALLENGING AND REPLACING PROCRASTINATION HABITS

Procrastination is often a habit in itself, which can be challenged and replaced with more productive behaviors:

- **Identify triggers:** Recognize what triggers your procrastinatory behavior. It could be a specific environment, an emotion, or even a time of day.

- **Replace responses:** After identifying triggers, consciously replace procrastinatory responses with more productive ones. For example, if you tend to procrastinate when you feel overwhelmed, try breaking the task into smaller chunks.

MAINTAINING HEALTHY HABITS

Maintaining healthy habits requires constant attention and adjustments. Be aware of how your habits evolve over time and be willing to adapt them as your needs and goals change.

Now that you understand the power of habits and how they can be shaped to combat procrastination, the next step is to learn how to prioritize tasks effectively. In the next chapter, " **PRIORIZATION TECHNIQUES** ," we'll explore methods to help you identify what needs your immediate attention and what can wait, allowing you to maximize each day to its full potential.

Are you ready to continue your journey to a more structured, less procrastinating life? Let's together explore how effectively prioritizing your tasks can make a significant difference to your productivity and overall satisfaction.

PRIORITIZATION TECHNIQUES

Prioritizing effectively is essential to managing your time and tasks in a way that maximizes your productivity and minimizes procrastination. This chapter covers practical methods to help you identify the most important and urgent tasks, ensuring you dedicate your energy where it is needed most.

THE IMPORTANCE OF PRIORITIZING

Without clear prioritization, it's easy to get lost in a sea of tasks, often dedicating time to less important activities to the detriment of those that truly advance your goals. Prioritizing helps ensure that you are always working on the projects that provide the greatest return for your efforts.

PRIORITIZATION METHODS

Let's explore some effective techniques you can incorporate into your daily routine to improve your ability to prioritize:

Eisenhower Matrix:

- **Important and urgent:** Tasks you need to do immediately.

- **Important but not urgent:** Tasks that you should schedule to do later.

- **Not important, but urgent:** Tasks that you should delegate.

- **Not important and not urgent:** Tasks that you can eliminate.

ABCDE Method:

- **A (very important):** Tasks that have serious consequences if not carried out.

- **B (important):** Tasks that have moderate consequences.

- **C (not very important):** Tasks that have minor

consequences.

- **D (delegable):** Tasks that can be passed on to someone else.

- **E (eliminable):** Tasks that do not need to be done.

80/20 Rule (Pareto Principle):

- This rule suggests that 80% of results come from 20% of activities. Identify and focus on those activities that generate the greatest results.

Applying prioritization techniques

- **Review daily:** At the end of each day, review and prioritize tasks for the next day. This helps ensure you start with the most critical tasks.

- **Be flexible:** Priorities can change quickly, so it's important to maintain the flexibility to adjust your to-do list as needed.

INTEGRATION WITH PRODUCTIVITY HABITS

Effectively prioritizing your tasks should become a habit that complements other productivity techniques you are already practicing, such as time management and goal setting. Coherence between these practices amplifies their effects and maximizes efficiency.

Now that you are equipped with techniques to effectively prioritize your tasks, the next chapter, " **CREATING AN ENVIRONMENTAL ENVIRONMENT** ," will explore how to organize your physical and digital space to support your priorities and maximize productivity. Creating a suitable environment can be the final element that will solidify your efforts against procrastination.

Are you ready to take the next step and learn how a well-organized environment can make all the difference in your ability to follow your priorities? Let's discover together how you can transform your space to reflect and facilitate your most important goals.

CREATING AN ENVIRONMENTAL ENVIRONMENT

A well-organized environment can do wonders for your productivity and focus, reducing distractions and making it easier to adopt good work habits. This chapter discusses how you can organize your physical and digital space in a way that supports your priorities and maximizes your efficiency.

THE INFLUENCE OF THE ENVIRONMENT ON BEHAVIOR

The environment around us can have a significant impact on our behavior. A disorganized space can contribute to procrastination, while an orderly, stimulating environment can encourage action and improve concentration.

ORGANIZING PHYSICAL SPACE

- **Minimize distractions:** Eliminate items from your work area that are not essential to your current tasks. This includes visual disorders that can divert your attention.

- **Define work zones:** Separate your workspace into specific areas for different activities. For example, one area for computing, another for reading, and one for meetings or brainstorming.

- **Personalize with intention:** Decorate your space in a way that reflects your goals and inspires motivation. This could include motivational quotes, a vision board, or even a color setting that you find energizing.

ORGANIZING THE DIGITAL ENVIRONMENT

- **Desktop and browser cleaning:** Keep your desktop and browser clean by organizing files and closing tabs that are no longer needed. Use file management tools and bookmarks to keep everything accessible.

- **Controlled notifications:** Configure your notifications to minimize interruptions. This may involve disabling pop-ups or setting a specific time to check emails and messages.

- **Productivity tools and apps:** Use apps that help you stay organized and productive, such as calendars, to-do lists, and distracting website blockers.

TIPS FOR ENVIRONMENTAL MAINTENANCE

- **Regular review:** Take time regularly to review and adjust your workspace. This could be daily, weekly or monthly depending on your needs.

- **Cleaning habit:** Develop the habit of cleaning your space at the end of each work day, preparing it for a new productive day.

With your environment now set up to promote maximum efficiency, the next chapter, " **THE ROLE OF MOTIVATION** ", will explore how to find and nurture intrinsic and extrinsic motivations to maintain your productivity. Understanding and harnessing your motivation can be the key to staying consistent in your actions and avoiding procrastination.

Are you ready to continue this journey and delve deeper into the dynamics of motivation? Let's discover together how to maintain momentum and turn motivation into continuous action.

THE ROLE OF MOTIVATION

Motivation is the force that drives us to start and continue tasks until completion, even in the face of obstacles. This chapter explores how to understand and utilize both intrinsic and extrinsic motivation to maintain productivity and combat procrastination effectively.

UNDERSTANDING INTRINSIC AND EXTRINSIC MOTIVATION

Motivation can be divided into two main types: intrinsic and extrinsic. Intrinsic motivation comes from within, it is the motivation generated by the pleasure and personal satisfaction that an activity provides. On the other hand, extrinsic motivation is driven by external factors such as material rewards or recognition from others.

- **Intrinsic motivation:** Involvement in activities that are intrinsically rewarding, not requiring external rewards. Examples include hobbies or personal projects that you find interesting and challenging.

- **Extrinsic motivation:** Includes factors such as salaries, promotions, course grades or even praise and social approval. Although effective, these factors may not sustain long-term motivation if there is no personal interest in the task.

FOSTERING INTRINSIC MOTIVATION

Intrinsic motivation is often more sustainable and can be strengthened by the following methods:

- **Set personal goals:** Set goals that align with your personal interests and passions. This increases the personal relevance of tasks and, consequently, your engagement and dedication.

- **Seeking new challenges:** Seeking challenges can rejuvenate your interest and commitment to your activities, especially if they are aligned with your personal goals and aspirations.

- **Self-reflection:** Take time regularly to reflect on what you love to do and why it is important to you, reinforcing your emotional connection to your tasks.

USING EXTRINSIC MOTIVATION EFFECTIVELY

While intrinsic motivation is ideal, extrinsic motivation should not be neglected. It can be particularly useful in tasks that are less interesting but necessary:

- **Tangible rewards:** Establish rewards for completing specific tasks. For example, if you finish an important report, you can treat yourself to dinner out or a new book.

- **Positive feedback:** Seek regular feedback, which can not only offer external encouragement but also valuable insights into how to improve your performance.

- **Supportive environment:** Create or participate in an environment that values and recognizes effort and success, which can significantly increase your motivation to stay productive.

Now that you understand how motivation works and how it can be optimized, the next step is to explore tools and resources that can help you apply and maintain motivation on a daily basis. In the next chapter, " **TOOLS AND RESOURCES AGAINST PROCRASTINATION** ", we will discuss practical applications and strategies that can help combat procrastination.

Are you ready to add these tools to your arsenal and ensure your motivation stays high? Let's together discover the best practices and technologies that can transform the way you face your daily tasks.

TOOLS AND RESOURCES AGAINST PROCRASTINATION

Modern technology offers a multitude of tools and resources that can be used to effectively combat procrastination. This chapter explores some of the best applications, techniques and strategies that you can incorporate into your daily life to maintain productivity and minimize putting off important tasks.

APPLICATIONS AND DIGITAL TOOLS

Time Management Apps:

- **Trello** : Ideal for organizing projects into boards and lists, making it easier to see the progress of tasks.

- **Todoist** : A to-do list app that lets you create daily tasks and projects with deadlines and priorities.

Focus Tools:

- **Forest:** This app helps you stay focused by encouraging you not to touch your phone. Planting a virtual tree that grows while you work can be a great motivator.

- **Freedom** : Blocks distracting websites and apps for a set period of time, helping you stay focused on tasks.

Habit tracking software:

- **Habitica** : Turns your daily tasks and habits into a role-playing game, where you can "level up" by completing tasks and forming good habits.

- **Streaks** : This app is useful for building and maintaining habits, allowing you to track your progress and maintain motivating streaks.

PRACTICAL TECHNIQUES TO REDUCE PROCRASTINATION

- **Pomodoro Technique:** As mentioned previously, it consists of working for 25 minutes straight and taking a 5-minute break. This helps maintain energy and motivation throughout the day.

- **Minimum viable goals:** Establish the least effort required to start a task. The simple act of starting can often lead to completing the entire task.

- **Two-minute method:** If a task can be done in two minutes or less, do it immediately. Quickly eliminating small tasks can significantly reduce your to-do list.

CREATING A SUPPORT SYSTEM

- **Accountability Groups:** Join or form accountability groups where members regularly share progress and encourage each other.

- **Coaching or mentoring:** Having someone to guide, motivate and offer feedback can be extremely valuable in overcoming procrastination and achieving bigger goals.

Now equipped with practical tools and tips to overcome procrastination, the next step is to understand how mindfulness and self-awareness can further improve your ability to manage your time and tasks. In the next chapter, " **MINDFULNESS AND SELF-AWARENESS** ," we'll explore how mindfulness techniques can help you recognize and control procrastinatory impulses.

Are you ready to deepen your understanding of yourself and improve your productivity through mindfulness? Let's discover together how these practices can transform your approach to work and daily life.

MINDFULNESS AND SELF-AWARENESS

Mindfulness is a powerful practice that helps increase self-awareness and manage emotions, making it a valuable tool for combating procrastination. This chapter explores how mindfulness can help you recognize and control procrastinatory impulses, and how cultivating greater self-awareness can transform your productivity and overall well-being.

UNDERSTANDING MINDFULNESS

Mindfulness involves maintaining a moment-to-moment awareness of our thoughts, feelings, bodily sensations, and surrounding environment, through a gentle, non-judgmental lens. This practice allows us to observe our habits and behaviors more objectively, which is essential for recognizing and modifying procrastination patterns.

BENEFITS OF MINDFULNESS IN REDUCING PROCRASTINATION

- **Increased self-awareness:** By practicing mindfulness, you become more aware of the reasons underlying your tendency to procrastinate, be it anxiety, fear or lack of motivation.

- **Stress management:** Mindfulness helps reduce stress levels, which can lessen the tendency to put off tasks due to anxiety or overwhelm.

- **Improved focus:** Regularly practicing mindfulness increases your ability to focus on one task at a time, reducing the distraction that often leads to procrastination.

PRACTICAL MINDFULNESS TECHNIQUES

- **Sitting meditation:** Dedicate a few minutes of your day to sit in silence and observe your breathing or repeat a mantra. This can help train your mind to focus and reduce distraction.

- **Breathing exercises:** Simple breathing techniques can be used to calm the mind and body, especially useful when you feel overwhelmed or unsure about starting a task.

- **Mindfulness during tasks:** Try to be completely present while carrying out an activity, even if it is something routine like washing the dishes or walking. This helps cultivate a habit of being fully engaged in the present moment.

DEVELOPING SELF-AWARENESS THROUGH SELF-REFLECTION

In addition to regular mindfulness practice, developing self-awareness through reflection can be extremely helpful:

- **Self-reflection journal:** Keep a journal to reflect on your daily experiences, thoughts and emotions. Identify which activities trigger procrastination and why.

- **Third-party feedback:** Asking for regular feedback from colleagues, friends, or mentors can provide outside insights into your behavior patterns, including procrastination.

Equipped with mindfulness and self-awareness techniques, the next step is to address how perfectionism can lead to procrastination and strategies for overcoming it. In the next chapter, " **OVERCOMING PERFECTIONISM** ," we'll explore how to adjust your expectations and approaches to prevent the pursuit of perfection from becoming an obstacle to productivity.

Are you ready to face and dismantle the barriers of perfectionism that may be hindering your progress? Let's learn together to balance excellence with efficiency in a practical and healthy way.

OVERCOMING PERFECTIONISM

Perfectionism, although it may seem like an admirable trait, often acts as a significant barrier to productivity, leading to procrastination. This chapter examines how perfectionism can manifest as a hindrance and offers practical strategies for overcoming this tendency by balancing the pursuit of excellence with a more functional and healthy approach to work and personal life.

UNDERSTANDING PERFECTIONISM

Perfectionism is the tendency to set unattainably high standards and strive for goals that are often unrealistic. This behavior can result in a paralyzing fear of making mistakes, which paradoxically can prevent projects from being completed or even started.

IMPACTS OF PERFECTIONISM

- **Procrastination:** Often, perfectionists put off tasks for fear of not being able to do the job perfectly.

- **Stress and anxiety:** The pressure to meet unrealistic standards can cause significant stress and anxiety.

- **Chronic dissatisfaction:** Perfectionists may feel constantly dissatisfied with their work, regardless of the quality, because they always think it could be better.

STRATEGIES TO OVERCOME PERFECTIONISM

- **Redefine your standards:** Start by adjusting your standards to more realistic and attainable levels. Recognize that "done is better than perfect" and that absolute perfection is a myth.

- **Focus on the process, not just the product:** Shift the focus from the result to the process of learning and growth. Value mistakes as essential opportunities for personal and professional development.

- **Division of tasks:** Break large projects into smaller, manageable parts. Set intermediate goals and celebrate small successes, which can reduce the pressure to perfect at each stage.

- **Practice self-compassion:** Cultivate an attitude of kindness towards yourself. Recognize that making mistakes is human and that imperfection is part of the human condition.

- **Set time limits:** Setting time limits for tasks can help avoid overthinking and the need to review work repeatedly.

Now that you have tools to combat perfectionism, the next chapter, " **SMALL STEPS TO BIG CHANGES** ," will explore how the technique of breaking big tasks into smaller chunks can be used to not only overcome procrastination, but also to bring about significant change and change. sustainable in your life.

Are you ready to take small steps that will lead to big changes? Let's discover together how to approach each project and each day in a strategic and satisfying way, maximizing productivity without sacrificing mental health.

SMALL STEPS TO BIG CHANGES

Adopting the strategy of dividing large tasks into smaller parts is an effective technique for combating procrastination and facilitating time management. This chapter explores how the "baby steps" approach can turn daunting projects into manageable task sequences, promoting not only task completion but also the development of healthier, more productive work habits.

THE PSYCHOLOGY BEHIND SMALL STEPS

When faced with big projects or goals, it's common to feel overwhelmed or intimidated, which can lead to procrastination. Breaking work down into smaller components helps reduce the anxiety associated with the workload, making the process more digestible and less threatening.

BENEFITS OF TASK DIVISION

- **Stress Reduction:** When tackling small parts of a larger task, stress and pressure are significantly reduced as each segment feels more doable.

- **Sense of progress:** Completing small tasks provides an immediate sense of progress and achievement, which can increase motivation to continue.

- **Improved focus:** Fewer elements competing for your attention allow for a more intense focus on each task, improving the quality of the work produced.

- **Facilitating planning:** It is easier to plan and adjust deadlines when work is organized into smaller segments.

IMPLEMENTING THE SMALL STEPS STRATEGY

- **Identify the end goal:** Start with a clear understanding of the desired outcome for the project or task.

- **Divide the project:** Break the larger objective into subgoals or phases that can be completed in sequence or in parallel.

- **Set realistic deadlines:** Assign specific deadlines for each small task, ensuring enough time to complete without unnecessary pressure.

- **Celebrate achievements:** Recognize and celebrate each small success along the way, which can reinforce positive behavior and encourage continued effort.

PRACTICAL EXAMPLE

Suppose you have to prepare a big presentation for work. Starting the project can seem daunting. Dividing the task:

- **Initial survey** (1-2 days)

- **Presentation outline** (1 day)

- **Slide development** (3-4 days)

- **Review and practice** (2-3 days)

Each step is clearly defined and feels more manageable, reducing the tendency to procrastinate.

Now that you're familiar with the strategy of breaking down tasks into smaller components, the next step is to understand how to set and manage deadlines effectively. In the next chapter, " **THE IMPACT OF DEADLINES** ," we'll explore how deadlines can be used to not only drive task completion, but also to improve the quality of work and avoid procrastination.

Are you ready to learn how to use deadlines to your advantage and turn time pressure into a productive ally? Let's discover how effective deadline management can be fundamental to the success of your projects.

THE IMPACT OF DEADLINES

Deadlines are a double-edged sword: on the one hand, they can be a significant source of stress and anxiety; on the other, they are essential tools for structuring our time and ensuring that tasks and projects are completed. This chapter explores how deadlines can be managed and used strategically to improve productivity and combat procrastination.

THE PSYCHOLOGY OF DEADLINES

Deadlines create a sense of urgency, which can motivate action. They function as a fixed reference point in the future that forces us to plan how we will use our time until then. However, if managed poorly, deadlines can also lead to stress and procrastination, especially if they seem unrealistic or overwhelming.

BENEFITS OF WELL ESTABLISHED DEADLINES

- **Clarity of objectives:** Clear deadlines help define the scope of a project and the pace necessary for its completion.

- **Effective prioritization:** With deadlines, it is easier to identify which tasks require immediate attention and which can wait, helping to better organize your time.

- **Increased motivation:** The proximity of a deadline can be a powerful motivator, leading to more intense focus and targeted action.

- **Preventing procrastination:** Firm deadlines help combat the tendency to procrastinate, establishing a time limit that encourages the beginning and completion of tasks.

STRATEGIES FOR MANAGING DEADLINES

- **Set realistic deadlines:** When setting deadlines, carefully consider the time needed to complete a task without rushing or compromising quality.

- **Break big deadlines into smaller ones:** Just like breaking big projects into smaller tasks, breaking a big deadline into several smaller ones can make the process less intimidating and more manageable.

- Use alerts and reminders: Set up regular reminders to stay aware of approaching deadlines, which can help keep the project on track.

- Review and adjust deadlines when necessary: If you notice that a deadline has become impractical, adjust it rather than forcing yourself to meet an unrealistic goal, which could lead to poor-quality work and increased stress.

TIPS FOR DEALING WITH DEADLINE PRESSURE

- Planning ahead: Start working on tasks well in advance of their deadlines whenever possible.

- Relaxation strategies: Incorporate mindfulness techniques and breathing exercises to manage stress related to deadline pressure.

- Effective communication: If you are working in a team or depend on others to meet deadlines, maintain clear and frequent communication to avoid misunderstandings and delays.

Understanding how to use deadlines to your advantage is just one part of combating procrastination. In the next chapter, " **BUILDING EMOTIONAL RESILIENCE** ," we'll explore how to strengthen your ability to deal with emotional challenges that can arise when facing deadlines and work pressures.

Are you ready to learn how to develop greater resilience that will help you face not just deadlines, but any challenge with confidence? Let's take the journey further to discover how to cultivate your inner strength and turn stress into a drive for success.

BUILDING EMOTIONAL RESILIENCE

Emotional resilience is the ability to recover quickly from difficulties and adapt well to adversity and stress. In this chapter, we will cover how to develop this resilience, essential for facing procrastination, managing deadlines and overcoming daily challenges at work and in your personal life.

THE IMPORTANCE OF EMOTIONAL RESILIENCE

Emotional resilience not only helps you deal with stress, but it also strengthens your ability to face challenges, make decisions under pressure, and persist in the face of obstacles. Developing this quality can transform the way you react to situations, leading to better results and greater personal satisfaction.

COMPONENTS OF EMOTIONAL RESILIENCE

- **Self-knowledge:** Recognizing your emotions and understanding how they influence your behavior is the first step towards resilience.

- **Positivity:** Maintaining a positive attitude, even in the face of difficulties, can change the perception of challenges and boost motivation.

- **Flexibility:** Being able to adapt to changes and adjust plans in response to unexpected situations is crucial to resilience.

- **Social support:** Having a reliable support network to turn to in times of need helps relieve stress and strengthen emotional resilience.

STRATEGIES FOR DEVELOPING EMOTIONAL RESILIENCE

- **Mindfulness and meditation:** Regular mindfulness practices can increase awareness of one's emotions and help manage responses to stress.

- **Setting limits:** Learning to say no and set healthy limits protects your emotional energy and prevents burnout.

- **Developing coping skills:** Identify and practice effective coping techniques, such as breathing techniques, physical exercise or relaxing hobbies.

- **Reflection and continuous learning:** Use past experiences as learning opportunities to improve your coping and resilience strategies.

IMPLEMENTING RESILIENCE IN EVERYDAY LIFE

- **Gratitude journal:** Keeping a journal where you write down things you are grateful for every day can reinforce positivity and perspective.

- **Regular exercise:** Regular physical activity not only helps reduce stress, but also promotes general well-being by strengthening emotional resilience.

- **Open communication:** Practice expressing your feelings and concerns in a healthy and productive way, whether with friends, family or therapists.

Now that you understand the importance of emotional resilience and how to develop it, the next step is to explore how feedback and support can be used to maintain accountability and encourage personal growth. In the next chapter, " **FEEDBACK AND SUPPORT** ," we will discuss how these elements are vital to continued success and how to effectively incorporate them into your professional and personal life.

Are you ready to further empower your personal growth journey with the help of constructive feedback and robust support? Let's go ahead and discover how these tools can enhance your ability to overcome challenges and achieve your goals.

FEEDBACK AND SUPPORT

Feedback and support are fundamental elements for any personal and professional growth process. This chapter explores how constructive feedback can help improve your skills and the importance of having a support network to maintain motivation and accountability on your journey to overcoming procrastination.

THE IMPORTANCE OF CONSTRUCTIVE FEEDBACK

Feedback is a valuable tool for personal and professional development. It provides external insights into performance, enabling continuous reflection and improvement. Constructive feedback helps you identify areas for improvement and celebrate successes, which is crucial for learning and growing.

TYPES OF FEEDBACK

- **Positive feedback:** Recognizes successes and reinforces behaviors that should be continued or repeated.

- **Constructive feedback:** Focuses on areas for improvement in a specific and useful way, offering practical suggestions for changes.

EFFECTIVELY IMPLEMENTING FEEDBACK

- **Be receptive:** Maintain an open attitude and consider feedback as an opportunity for growth.

- **Request feedback regularly:** Don't expect feedback only in formal reviews. Ask colleagues, friends or mentors for regular feedback on your performance.

- **Use feedback to establish goals:** Integrate the information received into your personal and professional development planning.

THE IMPORTANCE OF SUPPORT

Having a solid support network is essential for overcoming challenges and staying motivated. Support can come from a variety of sources, such as family, friends, coworkers, or professional support groups.

BUILDING AND MAINTAINING A SUPPORT NETWORK

> **- Engage in communities:** Join groups or communities that share similar interests or are facing similar challenges.

> **- Maintain regular communications:** Build and maintain relationships through regular communications, whether in person, over the phone or online.

> **- Be proactive:** Offer support to others, which can strengthen your relationships and create an environment of mutual support.

Feedback and support are essential, but knowing how to learn from mistakes is equally important. In the next chapter, "**LEARNING FROM MISTAKES** ," we'll explore how to turn failures and mistakes into powerful life lessons that can boost personal growth and reduce procrastination.

Are you ready to discover how to turn every mistake into a learning opportunity? We will move forward to understand how resilience is built not only through successes but also through failures, and how this can enrich your experience and effectiveness in all aspects of life.

LEARNING FROM MISTAKES

Viewing mistakes not as failures, but as essential learning opportunities, is crucial for personal and professional growth. This chapter explores how you can use mistakes to your advantage, turning each setback into a valuable lesson that boosts your development and overcoming procrastination.

THE INEVITABLE NATURE OF ERRORS

Errors are a natural and inevitable part of any trial and error process. The key to dealing with them effectively is not in avoiding mistakes at all costs, but in learning to react constructively when they occur.

BENEFITS OF LEARNING FROM MISTAKES

- **Continuous improvement:** Each error offers specific insights into how to improve your skills or approach in future attempts.

- **Reinforced resilience:** By learning to see mistakes as part of the learning process, you develop greater emotional resilience and less risk aversion.

- **Stimulated innovation:** Often, mistakes lead to new ideas and creative solutions that would not be considered in an unobstructed path.

STRATEGIES FOR LEARNING FROM MISTAKES

- **Reflective analysis:** After a mistake, take time to reflect on what happened. Ask yourself: What went wrong? What could be done differently? What can I learn from this?

- **Open discussion:** Share your mistakes with mentors, colleagues or friends for feedback. Open discussion can provide new perspectives and solutions that you may not have considered.

- **Implementing changes:** Use lessons learned to adjust your strategies or processes. This may involve changes to the way you plan projects, the way you manage your time, or the techniques you use to complete tasks.

CREATING AN ENVIRONMENT THAT ENCOURAGES EXPERIMENTATION

- **Culture of openness:** Promote an environment, whether at work or at home, where mistakes are seen as part of the learning process, not as failures to be punished.

- **Encouragement of calculated risk:** Encourage yourself and others to take calculated risks. This can help overcome the fear of error that often leads to procrastination.

Now that you understand how mistakes can be turned into learning, the next step is to explore how taking care of your physical well-being can influence your productivity and ability to deal with challenges. In the next chapter, " **NUTRITION AND EXERCISE** ", we will discuss how a healthy lifestyle can support your mental and physical health, boosting your efficiency and helping you combat procrastination.

Are you ready to continue this journey and discover how a healthy body can support a productive mind? Let's go ahead and explore how tweaks to your diet and exercise routine can make a big difference in your ability to learn from mistakes and move forward with confidence and vigor.

NUTRITION AND EXERCISE

Taking care of your physical well-being is essential to maintain not only your health, but also a high level of energy and a mental state conducive to combating procrastination. This chapter discusses how a balanced diet and a regular exercise routine can significantly improve your productivity and ability to deal with stress and anxiety.

THE IMPORTANCE OF PROPER NUTRITION

The food you eat plays a crucial role in how your brain works, affecting everything from your energy and focus to your mood. A poor diet can contribute to fatigue, irritability and a decreased ability to concentrate, while a balanced diet can increase your energy, mental clarity and work efficiency.

COMPONENTS OF A HEALTHY DIET

- **Complex carbohydrates:** Foods like whole grains provide long-lasting energy.

- **Lean proteins:** Sources such as fish, chicken, beans and nuts help build and repair tissues, in addition to being essential for brain function.

- **Healthy fats:** Omega-3 fats, found in fish and nuts, are important for brain health.

- **Fruits and vegetables:** Rich in vitamins, minerals and fiber, they contribute to general well-being and energy maintenance.

BENEFITS OF REGULAR EXERCISE

Exercise isn't just good for the body; it also has a significant impact on your mental health:

- **Stress reduction:** Physical activities help reduce stress levels and increase the production of endorphins, improving mood.

- **Improved concentration:** Regular exercise can help

improve cognitive function and memory.

- **Increased energy:** Staying active increases energy levels and combats fatigue, helping you to be more productive.

INTEGRATING NUTRITION AND EXERCISE INTO YOUR DAILY ROUTINE

- **Meal planning:** Prepare healthy meals and snacks in advance to avoid last-minute food choices that may be less healthy.

- **Set regular times for exercise:** Just like you plan other activities, make exercise a fixed part of your schedule.

- **Variety and fun:** Keep your exercise regimen interesting by varying activities; try walking, swimming, yoga or dancing.

Once you've established a solid foundation of nutrition and exercise, the next step is to explore meditation and relaxation techniques that can help clear your mind and further reduce procrastination. In the next chapter, " **MEDITATION AND RELAXATION** ," we will discuss how these practices can be integrated into your everyday life to improve focus, reduce stress, and cultivate a mental presence that promotes efficiency and productivity.

Are you ready to delve deeper into your self-care techniques and discover how a calm mind can be the key to a more productive, less procrastinated life? Let's explore the power of meditation and relaxation together

MEDITATION AND RELAXATION

In this chapter, we explore how meditation and relaxation techniques can be powerful tools for clearing the mind, reducing stress and anxiety, and combating procrastination. By integrating these practices into your daily life, you can significantly improve your focus and efficiency, as well as promote overall well-being.

BENEFITS OF MEDITATION FOR PRODUCTIVITY

Meditation has been linked to a variety of benefits that can directly impact your productivity:

- **Stress reduction:** Meditation helps reduce levels of cortisol, the stress hormone, promoting a feeling of calm and control.

- **Improved concentration:** Regular meditation practices can increase the duration and intensity of your focus.

- **Increased mental clarity:** Meditation helps to clear the mind of unnecessary thoughts, making it easier to organize ideas and prioritize tasks.

- **Emotional resilience:** Meditation strengthens the ability to deal with adversity, reducing impulsive reactions and procrastination resulting from negative feelings.

BASIC MEDITATION TECHNIQUES

- **Guided meditation:** Use guided meditation apps or videos, which provide step-by-step instructions through audio or text.

- **Mindfulness meditation:** Focus on observing your thoughts and sensations without judgment, bringing your attention back to your breathing whenever you become distracted.

- **Mantra meditation:** Repeat a specific mantra – a word or short phrase – to help you stay focused and calm.

RELAXATION TECHNIQUES

In addition to meditation, other relaxation techniques can help relieve physical and mental tension:

- **Breathing exercises:** Practices such as diaphragmatic breathing or 4-7-8 breathing can quickly calm the body and mind.

- **Progressive muscle relaxation:** Sequentially tense and relax different muscle groups, which can reduce anxiety and improve body awareness.

- **Guided Visualizations:** Imagine yourself in a peaceful, serene place, using all of your senses to intensify the experience and promote relaxation.

INTEGRATING MEDITATION AND RELAXATION INTO YOUR DAILY ROUTINE

- **Create a peaceful space:** Dedicate a space in your home exclusively for the practice of meditation and relaxation.

- **Establish a routine:** Determine a fixed time daily for your practices, which helps to form a consistent habit.

- **Small sessions:** Even short sessions of 5 to 10 minutes can be extremely beneficial, especially on busy days.

Now that you've learned how to meditate and relax, the next step is to recognize and celebrate your successes, a crucial step in maintaining motivation and momentum. In the next chapter, " **CELEBRATING SUCCESSES** ," we'll discuss how recognizing your advances can reinforce your commitment to productivity and continuous action.

Are you ready to step up and learn how to effectively celebrate each achievement on your journey? Let's discover together how to take advantage of each success to build an even more robust path towards your goals.

CELEBRATING SUCCESSES

Recognizing and celebrating your successes is essential for keeping motivation and energy high, as well as being a powerful tool against procrastination. This chapter addresses the importance of appreciating each victory on the path to your goals, offering practical strategies for integrating this celebration effectively and meaningfully into your life.

THE IMPORTANCE OF CELEBRATING SUCCESSES

Celebrating successes helps reinforce positive behaviors, increases self-esteem, and encourages continued effort toward greater goals. Furthermore, it provides moments of reflection, where you can evaluate what worked well and plan the next steps with greater confidence.

TYPES OF SUCCESSES TO CELEBRATE

- **Major achievements:** Completed projects, achieved goals, or major milestones deserve special recognition and celebration.

- **Small victories:** Don't underestimate the power of celebrating small daily victories, like completing a challenging task or maintaining consistency in a beneficial practice.

STRATEGIES FOR CELEBRATING SUCCESSES

- **Define clear criteria for success:** Establish upfront what constitutes success for you, whether it's completing a specific task, achieving a long-term goal, or improving a habit.

- **Appropriate celebrations:** Choose forms of celebration that are meaningful to you. This can range from a small personal treat to a leisure activity or party with friends and family.

- **Share your achievements:** Sharing your success with others can amplify a sense of accomplishment and provide external support and recognition.

- **Success Log:** Keep a success diary where you document your victories. This not only serves as a reminder of your capabilities, but also as a source of motivation in times of doubt or challenge.

CREATING A CELEBRATION CULTURE

- **Mutual encouragement:** Promote an environment where each person's success is celebrated. This can be particularly powerful in the workplace or in study groups and collaborative projects.

- **Regular recognition:** Implement a routine of regular recognition, both for yourself and others, to ensure that all efforts are appreciated.

Having established the importance of celebrating successes, the next chapter will focus on how periodically unplugging can benefit your productivity and overall well-being. In the chapter " **DISCONNECTING TO RECONNECT** ", we'll explore techniques for balancing technology use with moments of disconnection, allowing valuable time to recharge and reflect.

Are you ready to learn how a balance between connectivity and breaks can be crucial to sustainable success? Let's find out how to effectively implement periods of disconnection into your routine to maximize your mental clarity and focus.

DISCONNECTING TO RECONNECT

In the digital age, being constantly connected may seem essential, but regular periods of disconnection are crucial to maintaining a clear mind and a productive life. This chapter discusses the importance of periodically stepping away from digital technologies to improve focus, creativity, and overall well-being.

THE IMPORTANCE OF DISCONNECTING

Constant exposure to screens and social media can lead to information overload, reducing the ability to concentrate and increasing stress levels. Unplugging helps:

- Reduce anxiety and stress accumulated by excessive use of digital devices.

- Increase awareness and presence in the present moment.

- Improve the quality of interpersonal relationships, allowing for more meaningful and attentive interactions.

STRATEGIES TO EFFECTIVELY DISCONNECT

- **Establish clear limits:** Set specific times during the day to check emails and social media, and be strict about respecting them.

- **Scheduled disconnection:** Choose periods during the week or weekends to completely disconnect from all electronic devices.

- **Create technology-free routines:** Engage in activities that don't require technology, such as reading a book, practicing a manual hobby, or spending time in nature.

BENEFITS OF DISCONNECTING

- **Improved sleep quality:** Avoiding screens before bed can significantly improve your sleep, which is essential for good cognitive and physical performance.

- **Increased creativity:** Stepping away from the constant

input of information allows the mind to wander and explore new ideas.

- **Strengthening relationships:** Quality time without technological interruptions can strengthen bonds with friends and family.

IMPLEMENTING DISCONNECT INTO DAILY LIFE

- **Technology-free environments:** Create areas in your home that are technology-free zones, such as the bedroom or dining room.

- **Intentional technology use:** Make conscious choices about when and how to use technology, focusing on using it productively and limiting recreational use that does not add value.

- **Meditation and mindfulness:** Practice mindfulness techniques to cultivate greater presence, which can be especially helpful during times of disconnection.

After exploring the importance of disconnecting to reconnect, the next step is to establish start-of-work rituals that prepare your mind for a productive day. In the next chapter, " **STARTING WORK RITUALS** ", we will discuss how to create procedures that signal the start of focus on work and help you get into 'action mode'.

Are you ready to optimize your entry into work periods and maximize your productivity through effective rituals? Let's explore together how to start each workday on the right foot, ensuring that every moment of activity is as productive as possible.

STARTING WORK RITUALS

Establishing work start rituals is an effective strategy for signaling to your brain that it's time to shift focus from your personal life to your professional responsibilities. This chapter covers how to create and maintain rituals that help you get into "action mode," maximizing productivity and efficiency from the start of your workday.

THE IMPORTANCE OF STARTING WORK RITUALS

Commencement rituals help create a clear demarcation between personal and professional time, especially important in flexible work environments or home offices. These rituals can:

- Increase concentration and focus.

- Reduce procrastination.

- Establish a stable routine that can increase efficiency.

ELEMENTS OF AN EFFECTIVE BEGINNING RITUAL

- **Prepared workspace:** Before starting, ensure that your workspace is organized and free from distractions. This may include organizing necessary documents, preparing the workstation, and setting a clear to-do list.

- **Mindfulness or short meditation:** A few minutes of meditation or breathing exercises help to clear your mind and focus on the day's tasks.

- **Goal review:** Quickly reviewing the day's goals can reinforce what needs to be prioritized and help you stay focused on the most critical activities.

- **Energizing drink or food:** Starting the day with a nourishing ritual, such as a cup of coffee or tea, or a small breakfast, can be both a comfort and a form of energization.

IMPLEMENTING AND MAINTAINING STARTING RITUALS

- **Consistency:** The key to any ritual is consistency. Try to start your work the same way every day to establish and reinforce the habit.

- **Customization:** Tailor your start-up ritual to suit your personal needs and preferences. What works for one person may not be ideal for another.

- **Flexibility:** Be open to adjusting your ritual as needed, especially if you notice that certain elements are not helping to improve your productivity.

After establishing effective work-start rituals, the next step is to understand how to deal with the guilt associated with procrastination. In the next chapter, " **DEALING WITH GUILT** ," we'll explore strategies for overcoming feelings of guilt that can arise when tasks are put off, allowing you to move beyond setbacks with a more resilient, focused mindset.

Are you ready to face it and turn guilt into a motivating force that propels you forward, rather than letting it slow down your progress? Let's learn together to effectively manage these emotions to maintain productivity and emotional well-being.

DEALING WITH GUILT

The guilt associated with procrastination can be a major obstacle, generating feelings of inadequacy and demotivation. This chapter explores how to manage and overcome guilt so that it doesn't become a vicious cycle that perpetuates more procrastination.

UNDERSTANDING THE GUILT IN PROCRASTINATION

Guilt arises when we realize that we have not met our own expectations or the expectations of others. In the context of procrastination, this often translates into a feeling of failure for not starting or completing a task as planned. This emotion can be paralyzing and further harm productivity.

STRATEGIES FOR OVERCOMING GUILT

- **Recognition and acceptance:** Accept that procrastination is a human behavior and that feeling guilty about it, although common, is not productive. Recognizing and accepting your feelings of guilt is the first step to overcoming them.

- **Realistic analysis:** Realistically evaluate the situation that led to procrastination. Ask yourself whether the expectations for yourself were reasonable and whether there are external factors that influenced your ability to accomplish the task.

- **Learning and adjustment:** Use experience to learn. Analyze what can be improved, adjust your work methods or your planning, and consider this as an opportunity for growth, not a failure.

- **Positive self-talk:** Change your self-talk from criticism to positive affirmations. Instead of punishing yourself, remind yourself of your achievements and your ability to overcome challenges.

- **Set smaller goals:** Reset your tasks with smaller, more manageable goals that are easier to achieve and can help rebuild your confidence.

AVOIDING FUTURE GUILT

- **Proactive planning:** Plan your activities with time buffers for unforeseen events, which can help avoid subsequent procrastination and guilt.

- **Support and communication:** Communicate openly with coworkers, friends, or family about your struggles with procrastination. They can offer support, understanding, or even practical solutions.

- **Regular reflection:** Set aside time regularly to reflect on your work practices and emotional well-being. This can help you identify patterns of procrastination and develop strategies for dealing with them before guilt sets in.

Now that we've discussed strategies for dealing with guilt, the next and final chapter, " **TOWARDS ACTION** ," brings together all of the insights and techniques covered throughout the book to drive an ongoing commitment to productivity and action. This final chapter will serve as a guide to implementing and maintaining the changes necessary to turn procrastination into efficiency.

Are you ready to consolidate all your learning and transform it into concrete actions that will benefit your personal and professional life? Let's complete this journey together, equipped with tools and knowledge to face procrastination head-on and successfully.

TOWARDS ACTION

We have reached the last chapter of our journey through the book **"Beyond procrastination: transforming 'I'll do it later' into immediate action"** . Here, we will consolidate the insights and strategies discussed in previous chapters, establishing a clear and motivating plan to implement lasting changes that transform your tendency to procrastinate into a dynamic of ongoing efficiency and productivity.

REVIEW OF KEY POINTS

- **Understand procrastination:** We recognize the psychological and behavioral causes of procrastination and learn how this understanding can help us approach this challenge more effectively.

- **Coping Strategies:** We discuss several techniques for combating procrastination, including time management, setting clear goals, and developing healthy habits that promote action.

- **Emotional and social impact:** We explore how procrastination affects our emotional well-being and social relationships, and how building emotional resilience and supporting a network can strengthen our ability to take action.

IMPLEMENTING CHANGES

To truly transform the tendency to procrastinate into productive action, it is crucial to consistently apply the strategies discussed:

- **Set small, realistic goals:** Start with goals you know you can achieve and gradually challenge yourself with bigger goals.

- **Keep a progress diary:** Documenting your progress can not only motivate you to keep going, but also help you better understand patterns in your behavior.

- **Create successful routines:** Daily routines can help

automate productive behaviors, reducing the mental energy needed to start tasks.

CONTINUED COMMITMENT TO ACTION

- **Regular reassessment:** Take time regularly to review and adjust your action plan. This is vital to maintaining the relevance and effectiveness of the strategies you are using.

- **Seek constant feedback:** Feedback, whether from friends, family or co-workers, is essential to keep you on track and motivated.

- **Celebrate every success:** Recognize every small victory along the way. These celebrations reinforce your commitment to your goals and keep your energy high.

As you move forward, remember that the journey to overcoming procrastination is ongoing and evolving. Every step you take is a part of a larger process of self-discovery and personal growth. With the strategies and insights provided in this book, you are well-equipped to turn " **I'll do it later** " into " **immediate action** ." Continue to walk with confidence and determination, and you will find not only success in your tasks, but also a significant improvement in the quality of your life and work.

Are you ready to make action the norm, not the exception? Let's move forward, one step at a time, towards a more productive and fulfilled life.

As we turn the final page of this journey together, I sincerely hope that the learnings shared here have touched your heart and sparked new perspectives. If this book has brought you any value, I kindly ask that you take a few moments to leave a review on Amazon. Your words not only help me grow and hone my craft, but they also guide other readers in their quests for knowledge and inspiration. Your opinion is a valuable gift, both for me and for the community of readers looking for stories that transform. I sincerely thank you for sharing this journey with me and I hope we can meet again in the pages of a new adventure.

REGINALDO OSNILDO

Hello, I'm Reginaldo Osnildo, author and innovator in the areas of sales, technology, and communication strategies. My experience ranges from the academic environment, as a professor and researcher at the University of Southern Santa Catarina, to practice as a strategist at Grupo Catarinense de Rádios. With a PhD in sales narratives and digital convergence, and a master's degree in storytelling and social imaginary, I bring my readers a unique fusion of theory and practice. My goal is to provide knowledge in a simple, practical and didactic language, encouraging direct application in personal and professional life.

Yours sincerely

Reginaldo Osnildo

+55 48 991913865

reginaldoosnildo@gmail.com

www.ingramcontent.com/pod-product-compliance
Lightning Source LLC
Chambersburg PA
CBHW070351230526
45471CB00006B/2511